Going into Space

Carmel Reilly

Contents

Space

What would it be like to go into space?
What would it be like to see the Moon up close?

Orbit

We live on a **planet** called Earth. It is one of eight planets that **orbit** the Sun.

Some people have been to space. Some have walked on the Moon. There are even some people who are living in space right now!

Big Stars

Stars are huge! They only look tiny because they are very far away. Our Sun is a star. You could fit 1.4 million Earths inside the Sun.

Space in History

Thousands of years ago, people used the Sun, Moon, stars and planets to work out how to tell the time. This also helped them to work out the months and seasons of the year.

An ancient **astronomer** looks up at the stars.

Going to Space

People have looked up at the sky for thousands of years. But no one had ever been there.

That all changed in the 1950s. **Scientists** built rockets that went into space. Space travel is very dangerous, so the first rockets went to space without people in them.

This rocket was launched in 1958.

Laika

The very first space traveller was a dog called Laika. She was sent to space in a rocket in 1957. Sadly, Laika died not long after take-off.

The first **astronauts** travelled in rockets. Today, they travel in space shuttles.

a space rocket

In 1961, Yuri Gagarin became the first person to travel to space.

In 1969, Neil Armstrong became the first person to walk on the Moon.

Space in the Future

Space is a very, very big place. So far, people have been to a very small part of it. Astronauts have never been to other planets.

a space shuttle

Mars

The closest planet to Earth is Mars. Astronauts hope to go there by 2035.

Becoming an Astronaut

Becoming an astronaut is hard work. Astronauts have to study very hard at school and **university**.

Astronauts learn how to fly the space shuttle.

Then they spend many years learning about space travel. They learn about the space shuttle and the special **equipment** on board. They also have to be very fit and healthy.

Scientists make sure that astronauts are fit and healthy.

Accidents

Space travel can be dangerous. Twenty-two astronauts have died in accidents.

In 1986, the Space Shuttle Challenger exploded. Sadly, all astronauts onboard died.

Gravity

Gravity is what makes things fall to the ground. In space, there is very little gravity, so nothing falls. Everything just floats around – even people!

Astronauts are taller in space than they are on Earth. There is less gravity pushing down on their bodies. In space, astronauts stretch!

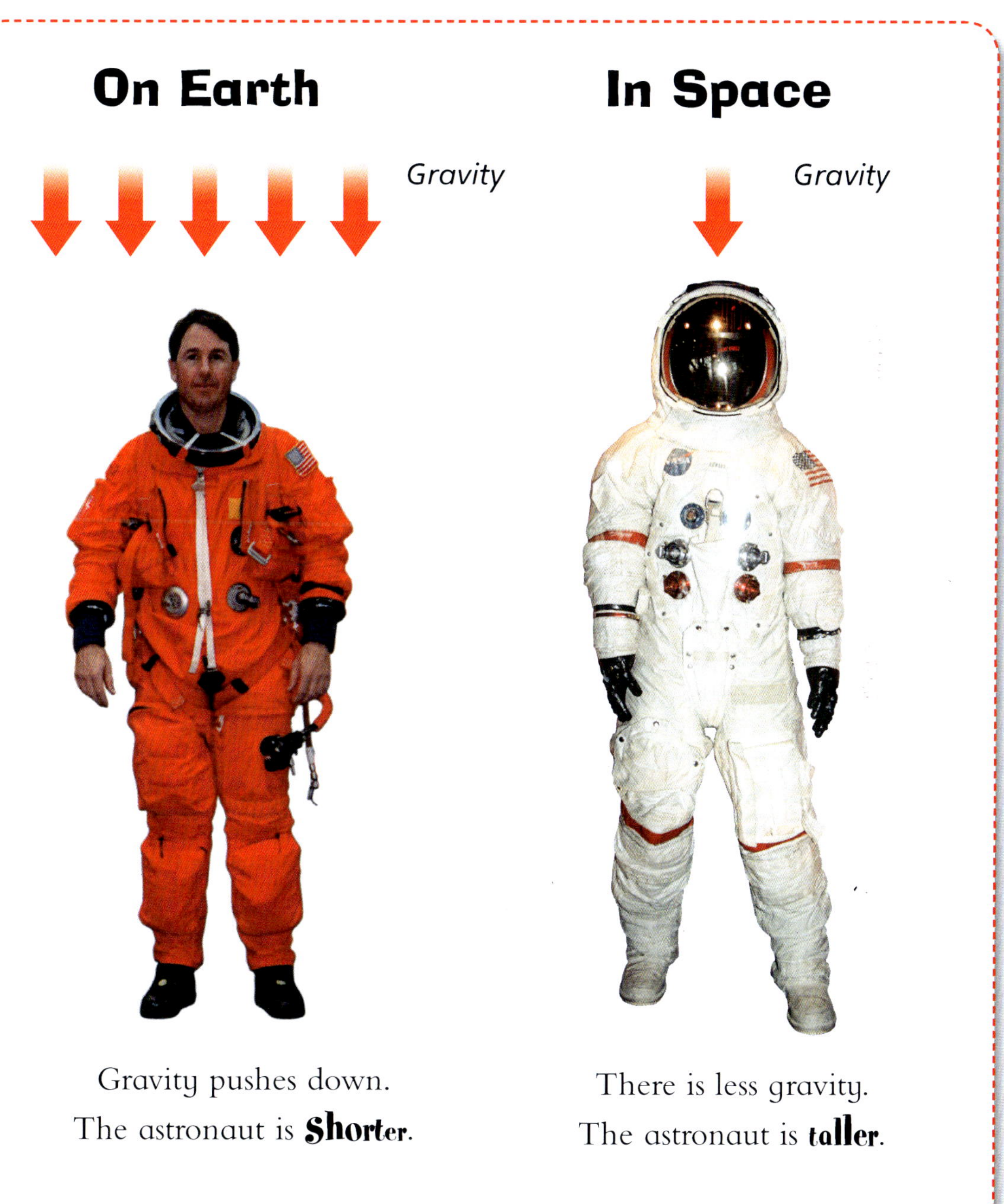

Gravity pushes down.
The astronaut is **shorter**.

There is less gravity.
The astronaut is **taller**.

Living in Space

When astronauts finish their training, they go on space **missions**. Some of these missions are short, but some can last for weeks or even months.

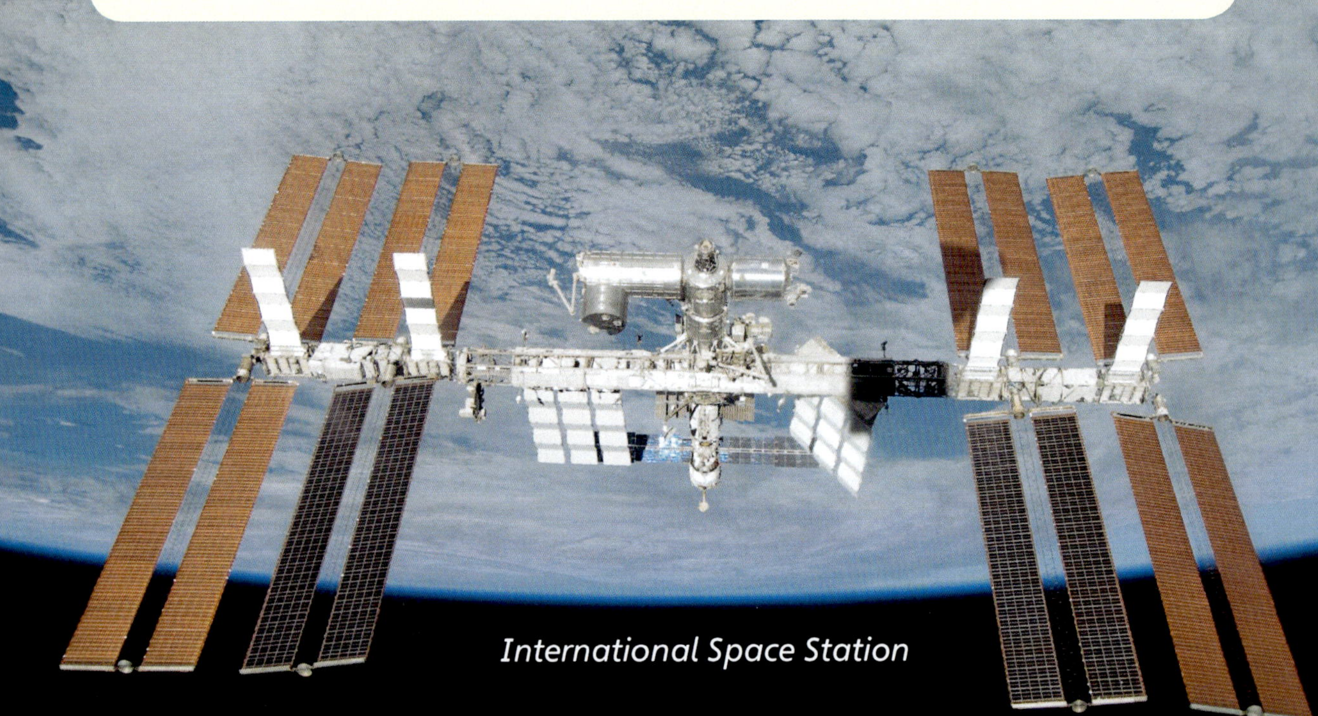

International Space Station

Space Stations

Astronauts on long missions live on the **International Space Station**. This is a special building in space.

	In the International Space Station
Kitchen	• microwaves • refrigerators • water • frozen food. Most of the food is cooked on Earth and frozen. Astronauts just have to re-heat it.
Bedrooms	• special beds to stop the astronauts from floating while they sleep • computers • lockers, to store clothes and other personal items
Bathroom	• toilet • towels • wet wipes and cloths, for washing
Gym	• treadmill • rowing machine • exercise bike
Laboratories	• machines, equipment and tools to carry out scientific **experiments** • computers

Building

The International Space Station is still being built. It was started in 1998 and will be finished in 2011. When it is finished, it will be like a big airport in space! Astronauts will stop there before going further into space.

Eating in Space

Imagine trying to eat if your food won't stay on the plate. Or if your water won't stay in the cup! That's what it's like when astronauts try to eat and drink in space.

An astronaut watches a blob of water floating through space.

Space Food

In the early days of space travel, an astronaut's food came in tubes, like toothpaste!

Watch Out for Those Crumbs!

Astronauts must make sure that bits of food, water and other rubbish do not float around the space station. Even the smallest crumbs could damage the equipment.

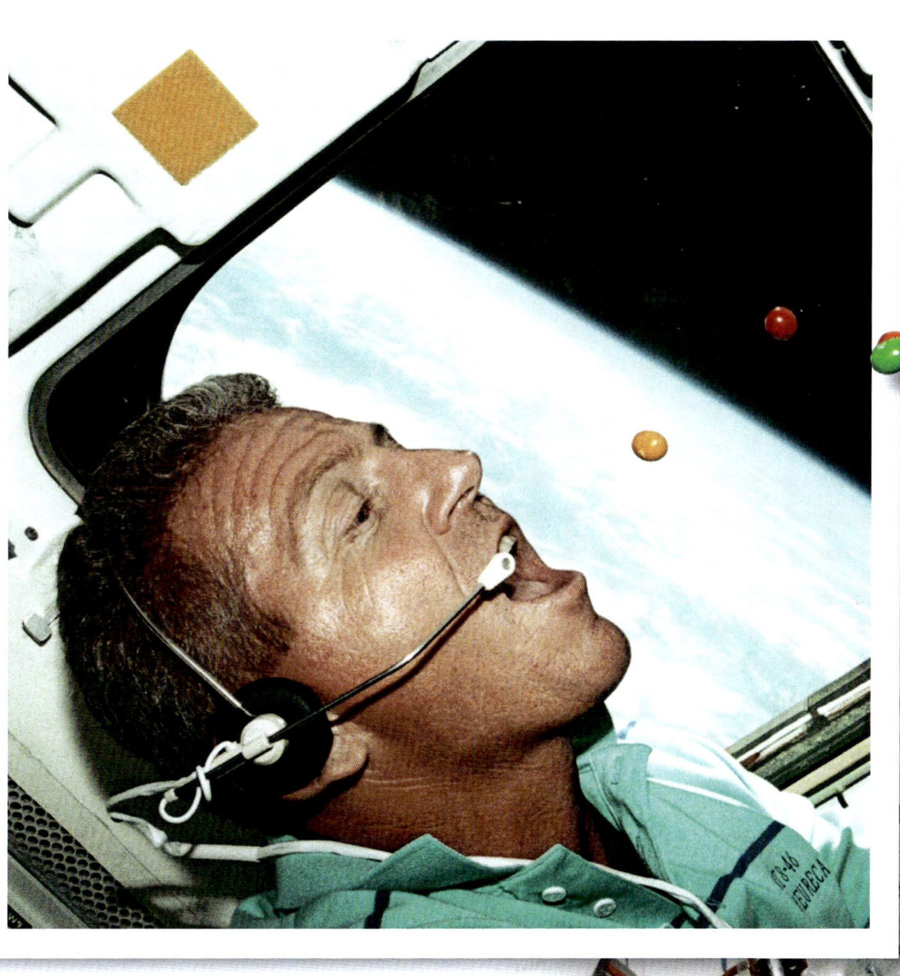

Eating floating chocolates in space!

Eating floating cookies!

Keeping Clean in Space

Astronauts don't take showers because the water would just float away. So they use wet cloths and wipes to keep clean.

This astronaut is washing his hair, in space!

Space Toilets!

Space stations have special toilets that suck waste safely away.

Water

Water is carried to the space station on a space shuttle. Astronauts have to be careful not to waste water.

All the waste produced at the space station is stored and taken back to Earth.

Working in Space

Astronauts don't go to space for a holiday! Each astronaut has important work to do.

Experiments

Astronauts look at how living in space affects their bodies. They also take plants into space and see how living in space affects them.

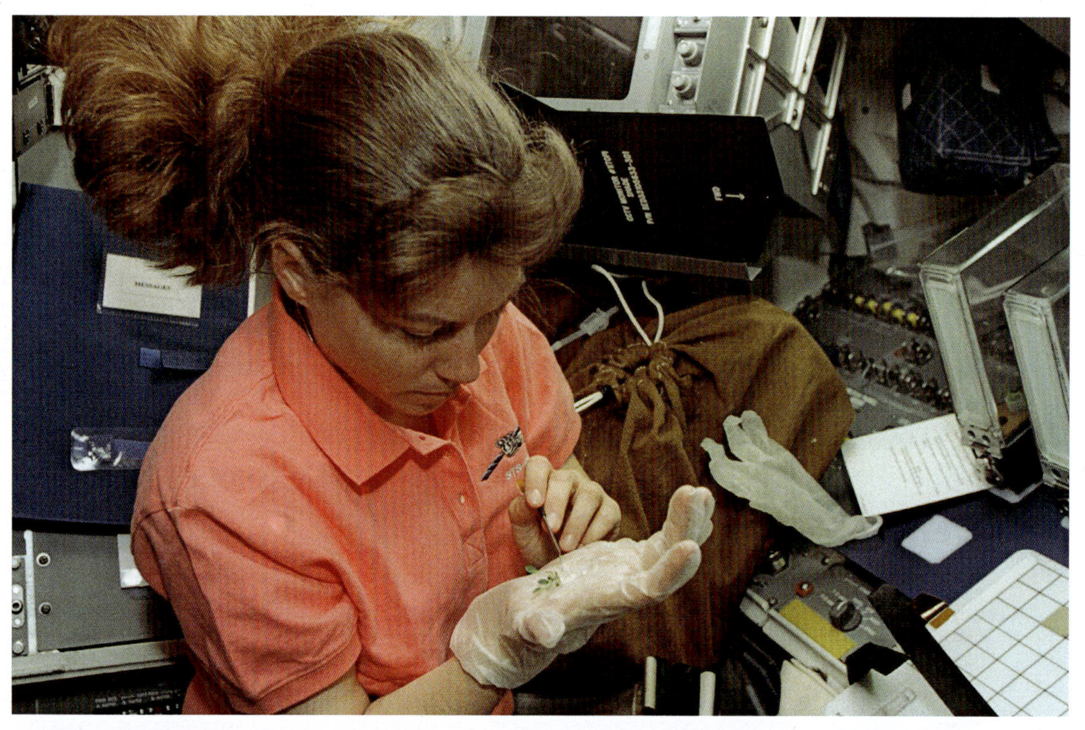

This astronaut is doing an experiment on a plant.

Astronauts also watch Earth from space. This helps them to learn more about things that happen on Earth, like fires or floods.

This astronaut is taking photos of space.

A view of Earth, from the flight deck of a space shuttle.

Walking in Space

Sometimes, parts of the space station need to be fixed. So astronauts have to go outside the space station. They walk in space!

This astronaut is working outside the space station.

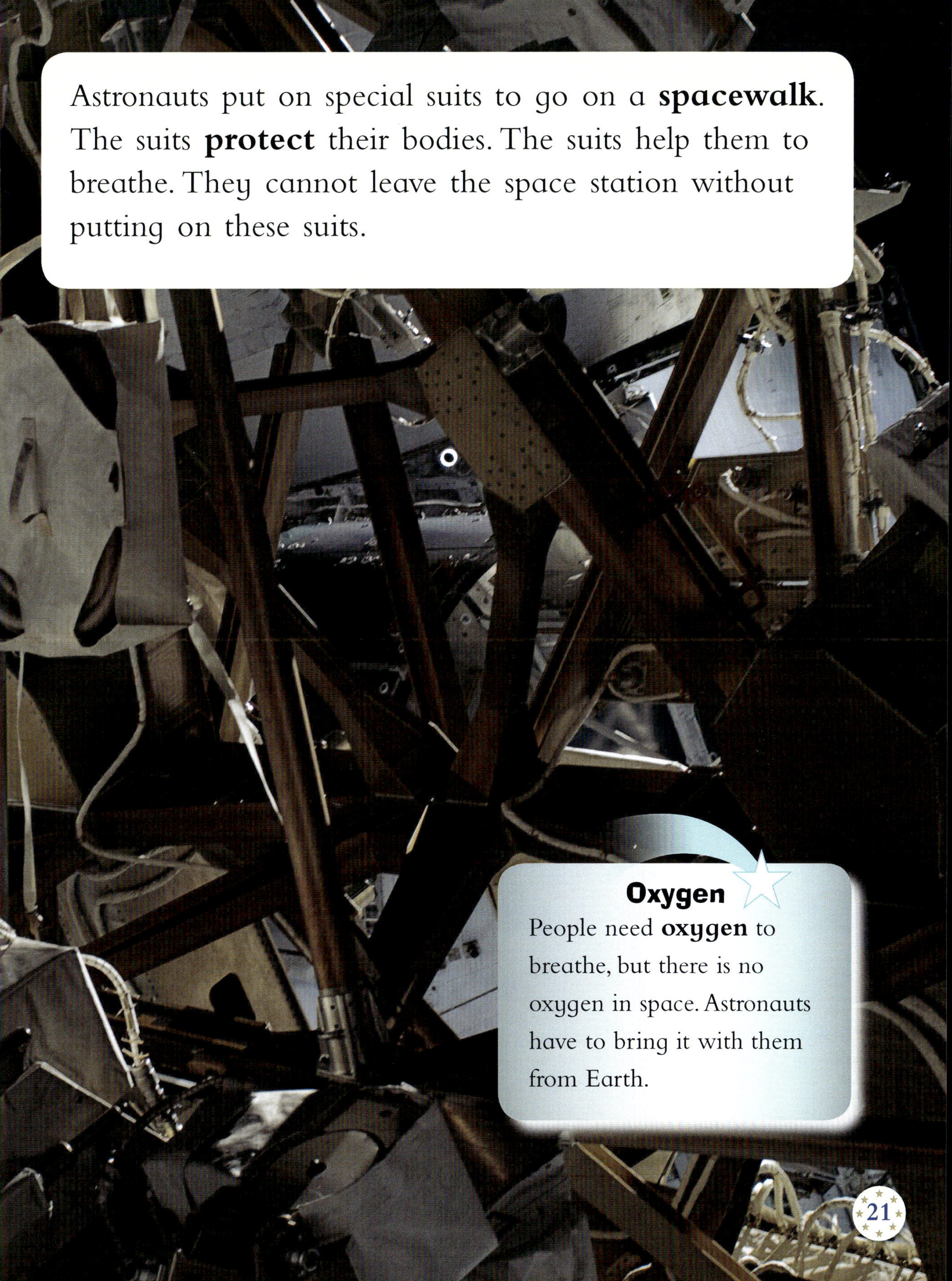

Astronauts put on special suits to go on a **spacewalk**. The suits **protect** their bodies. The suits help them to breathe. They cannot leave the space station without putting on these suits.

Oxygen

People need **oxygen** to breathe, but there is no oxygen in space. Astronauts have to bring it with them from Earth.

Spacesuits

helmet:
protects the head, and makes sure there is oxygen for the astronaut to breathe
earphones and microphone:
lets astronauts talk to each other
oxygen tanks:
carry the oxygen

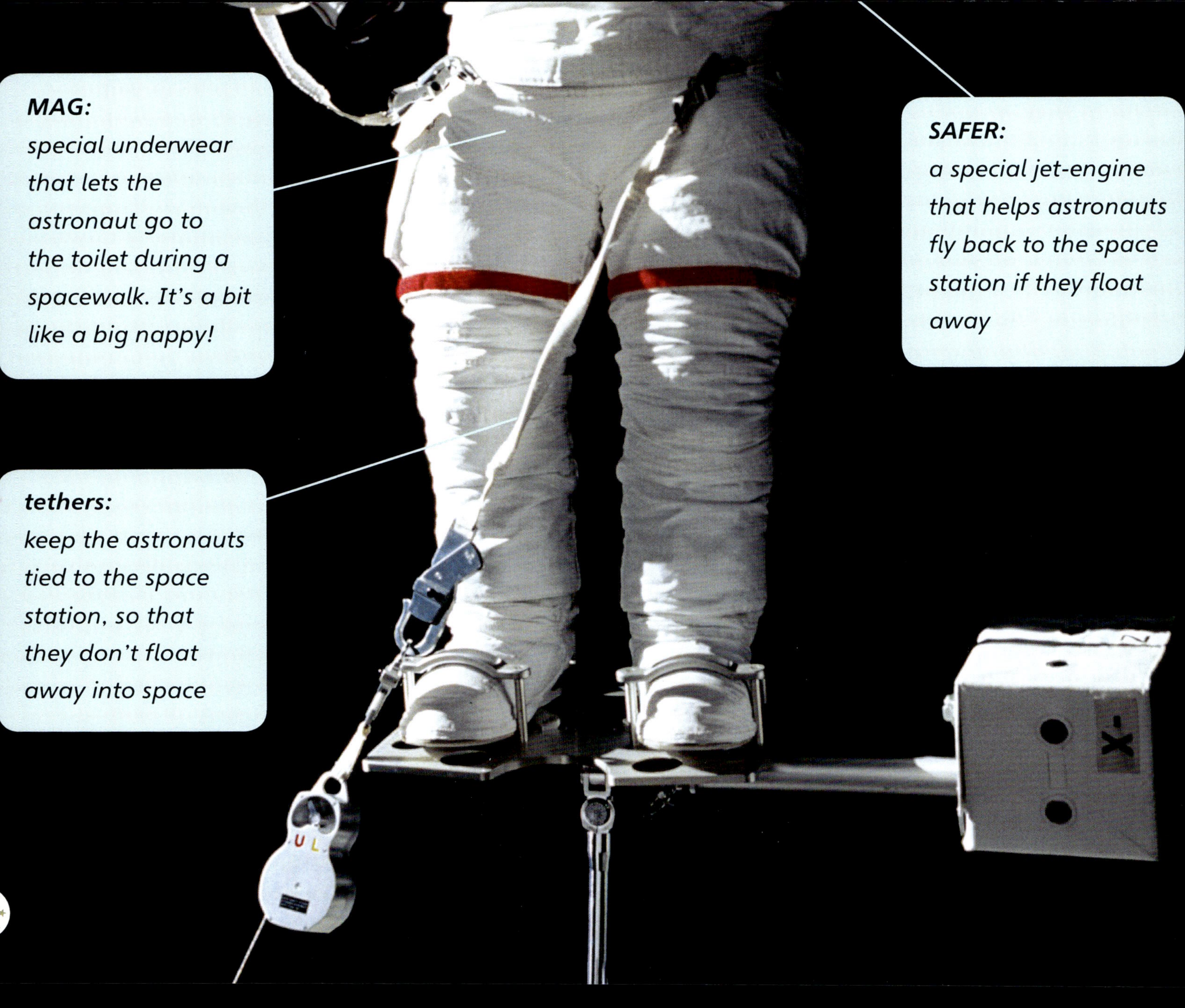
MAG:
special underwear that lets the astronaut go to the toilet during a spacewalk. It's a bit like a big nappy!
tethers:
keep the astronauts tied to the space station, so that they don't float away into space
SAFER:
a special jet-engine that helps astronauts fly back to the space station if they float away
-X

Resting in Space

Astronauts work hard in the space station, but they also need to relax. They need to take care of their bodies.

This astronaut is relaxing by reading in space.

Exercise

In space, astronauts exercise a lot. Back on Earth, gravity helps to keep our muscles and bones strong. In space, astronauts have to exercise more to make sure their bones and muscles stay strong.

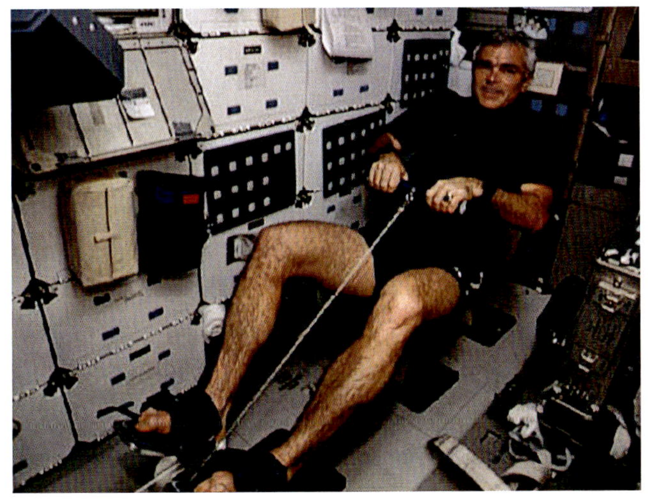

Exercising in space

Fitness training in space

Sleep

Sleeping in space is not easy. Sometimes, astronauts sleep standing up! And they have to be tied into sleeping bags to stop floating away while they sleep!

This astronaut is sleeping.

Day and Night, Night and Day

Days on the space station are much shorter than days on Earth. The Sun rises and sets every 90 minutes. This can make it hard to get a good night's sleep. By the time you drop off, it is morning again!

Days

On Earth, one day equals 24 hours. On the space station, there are 16 days every 24 hours!

Back to Earth

When astronauts have finished their mission, they take the space shuttle back to Earth.

The space shuttle flies towards Earth.

The space shuttle flies towards the landing strip.

After months in space, astronauts must learn how to live on Earth again. They may have forgotten what it's like to live with gravity! It can even be difficult for them to walk at first.

The back wheels touch down.

A parachute slows down the shuttle. The shuttle has landed!

Going to space is amazing – but it's always nice to come home again!

Space Fun

Space Spotting

Spot the four differences between these astronauts.

Answers

1. Red lens on camera; 2. missing NASA badge;
3. missing red band on leg; 4. missing black dot on bottom of jet pack.

Space Quiz

How much do you remember?

1. Have human beings walked on the Moon?

2. Which planet is closest to Earth?

3. Are astronauts taller on Earth or in space?

4. What makes objects fall to the ground on Earth?

5. How do astronauts wash themselves in space?

Answers

1. Yes 2. Mars 3. They are taller in space. 4. Gravity 5. They use wet cloths.

Glossary

astronauts
people who pilot spacecraft or work in space

astronomer
a person who studies objects in space

equipment
machines and tools that help people do their work

experiments
tests that help people learn more about the world

gravity
the force by which a planet pulls objects towards its centre

International Space Station
a large satellite that orbits Earth. It is so large that astronauts can live and work in it.

missions
tasks or jobs that astronauts are sent on

orbit
to move around something

oxygen
a gas that humans breathe to live

planet
an object in space that orbits around a star

protect
to keep safe

scientists
people who study and learn about the world around them

spacewalk
when an astronaut moves around and works outside the space station, in space

university
a place people go, after finishing high school, to do more study